Earthquakes
and Other Natural Disasters

FIRST EDITION
Editors Rachel Wardley, Steve Setford, and Lara Tankel; **Designer** Andrew Burgess;
Senior Editor Linda Esposito; **US Editor** Regina Kahney; **Deputy Managing Art Editor** Jane Horne;
Production Editor Siu Chan; **Picture Researcher** Angela Anderson; **Illustrator** Peter Dennis;
Reading Consultant Linda Gambrell, PhD

THIS EDITION
Editorial Management by Oriel Square
Produced for DK by WonderLab Group LLC
Jennifer Emmett, Erica Green, Kate Hale, *Founders*

Editors Grace Hill Smith, Libby Romero, Michaela Weglinski;
Photography Editors Kelley Miller, Annette Kiesow, Nicole DiMella; **Managing Editor** Rachel Houghton;
Designers Project Design Company; **Researcher** Michelle Harris; **Copy Editor** Lori Merritt;
Indexer Connie Binder; **Proofreader** Larry Shea; **Reading Specialist** Dr. Jennifer Albro;
Curriculum Specialist Elaine Larson

Published in the United States by DK Publishing
1745 Broadway, 20th Floor, New York, NY 10019
Copyright © 2023 Dorling Kindersley Limited
DK, a Division of Penguin Random House LLC
22 23 24 25 26 10 9 8 7 6 5 4 3 2 1
001-333883-May/2023

All rights reserved.

Without limiting the rights under the copyright reserved above, no part of this publication may be reproduced, stored in or introduced into a retrieval system, or transmitted, in any form, or by any means (electronic, mechanical, photocopying, recording, or otherwise), without the prior written permission of the copyright owner.
Published in Great Britain by Dorling Kindersley Limited

A catalog record for this book
is available from the Library of Congress.
HC ISBN: 978-0-7440-7149-8
PB ISBN: 978-0-7440-7150-4

DK books are available at special discounts when purchased in bulk for sales promotions, premiums, fundraising, or educational use. For details, contact: DK Publishing Special Markets,
1745 Broadway, 20th Floor, New York, NY 10019
SpecialSales@dk.com

Printed and bound in China

The publisher would like to thank the following for their kind permission to reproduce their images:
a=above; c=center; b=below; l=left; r=right; t=top; b/g=background

123RF.com: Sebastien Decoret 1b; **Alamy Stock Photo:** ART Collection 25crb, Artokoloro 11crb, peruvianpictures.com 43tr; **Dorling Kindersley:** Museo Archeologico Nazionale di Napoli / James Stevenson 14bl; **Dreamstime.com:** Fiona Ayerst 26clb, Binikins 3cb, Peter Bocklandt 40tl, Fmportella 17tr, Iofoto 35cr, Iurii Kuzo 13tr, Lavizzara 34cl, Richair 45t, Adriano Spano 15cr, Taras Vyshnya 44tl; **Getty Images:** E+ / TerryJ 45ctr, Fairfax Media 7bl, Hulton Archive / Print Collector 21tr, Moment / Feifei Cui-Paoluzzo 20bl, Moment / Sebastian Condrea 15tr; **Getty Images / iStock:** bluejayphoto 28clb, Wead 6br, 25tl; **NASA:** Johnson Space Center Gateway to Astronaut Photography of Earth 6tl; **Shutterstock.com:** Yvonne Baur 7crb

Cover images: *Front and Spine:* **Dreamstime.com:** Ollirg

All other images © Dorling Kindersley
For more information see: www.dkimages.com

For the curious
www.dk.com

Level 4

Earthquakes
and Other Natural Disasters

Harriet Griffey

CONTENTS

6	Powerful Planet
8	Vesuvius Erupts!
16	Lisbon's Great Quake
20	River of Sorrow
24	Pelée Awakes
28	Earthquake!

34	Long Island Express
40	Avalanche
44	Wildfire
46	Glossary
47	Index
48	Quiz

POWERFUL PLANET

Volcanoes, earthquakes, tidal waves, hurricanes, flash floods, and forest fires—nature running wild is both spectacular and terrifying.

Despite all our modern resources, natural disasters still devastate lives.

Long Island, NY (Hurricane, 1938) Fierce storm winds whipped up huge waves and ravaged the eastern coast of the United States. *See pages 34–39.*

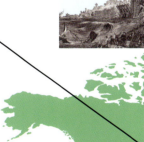

Lisbon, Portugal (Earthquake, 1755) Earth tremors and fires devastated Portugal's capital. *See pages 16–19.*

San Francisco, CA (Earthquake, 1906) The city was shaken to the ground and then consumed by fire. *See pages 28–33.*

Yungay, Peru (Avalanche, 1970) In the mountains of Peru, an avalanche of ice and rock buried the people of Yungay alive. *See pages 40–43.*

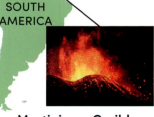

Martinique, Caribbean (Volcano, 1902) The terrible eruption of Mount Pelée destroyed the port of St. Pierre. *See pages 24–27.*

Every year they kill, injure, or leave homeless millions of people.

Here are the stories of some of the worst natural disasters in history. The map below tells you where the disasters occurred, and where you can find them in this book.

Hurricane Winds
These winds can rip trees from the soil, toss cars around as if they are toys, and tear roofs off buildings.

Pompeii, Italy
(Volcano, 79 CE) Mount Vesuvius erupted, burying the Roman town of Pompeii under layers of ash and mud. *See pages 8–15.*

Yellow River, China
(Flood, 1887) The Yellow River flooded China's Great Plain, killing two million people. *See pages 20–23.*

Southern Australia
(Bushfire, 1983) A severe drought caused fires to rampage across the Australian bush. *See pages 44–45.*

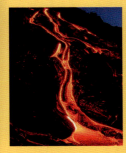

Lava Flow
Red-hot lava may ooze gently from a volcano or be thrown high into the air by the force of the eruption.

7

Vesuvius
People had no reason to fear the volcano—it had been quiet for 800 years.

Take-Out Food
At outdoor cafés, snacks were served from bowls sunk into the counter.

VESUVIUS ERUPTS!
Italy, 79 ce

It was a scorching-hot morning. At the foot of Mount Vesuvius, an inactive volcano in southern Italy, the Roman town of Pompeii baked in the August sunshine.

Despite the heat, Pompeii's streets and markets were bustling. The smell of fresh bread from bakers' ovens filled the air, and traveling musicians entertained the shoppers.

At a take-out restaurant, two women ordered snacks for their children. A man tied his dog to the counter and waited to be served.

8

In the packed taverns, people spoke excitedly about the afternoon's games in the amphitheater. This was a stadium where huge, bloodthirsty crowds gathered to watch trained warriors called gladiators fight each other—often to the death!

Just then, the ground trembled. The women at the take-out counter exchanged worried glances. Could it be another earthquake? They were common in the area but usually did little damage.

Suddenly there was a deafening boom—and the top of Mount Vesuvius blew right off!

Gladiator Helmet
Gladiators were criminals or enslaved people. The most successful fighters were granted their freedom.

Amphitheater
Gladiator fights and chariot races were held in Pompeii's amphitheater.

Blastoff!
Hot, liquid rock moved up through the volcano until it blasted through the top of the mountain.

Unlucky Wind
The force of the eruption broke the hot rock into billions of pieces of ash. Wind blew the deadly ash cloud toward Pompeii.

Mount Vesuvius was erupting! A fountain of fire shot upward and huge black clouds rose into the sky. The ground shook with the force of the explosion. People staggered, clinging tightly to one another.

The eruption of Vesuvius was similar to this 1980 eruption of Mount St. Helens in Washington State.

10

The women at the take-out restaurant pulled their children close. The dog barked wildly and strained at its lead. Taverns emptied and people ran from their homes, afraid to stay indoors in case the buildings collapsed.

Though it was daytime, darkness fell on Pompeii as ash and smoke blocked out the sun. Lightning bolts zigzagged through the towering cloud of ash above Vesuvius.

Smoldering ash and rocks—some the size of tennis balls—rained down from the sky. Crowds ran screaming through the gloomy streets, upsetting market stalls and trampling fruit and vegetables underfoot. Even gladiators training in the amphitheater dropped their weapons and ran.

Some people rushed to save precious objects. Others tied cushions or towels to their heads for protection as they fled the streets of Pompeii.

Eyewitness
A man named Pliny watched the eruption from a distance. This description is based on his eyewitness account of the disaster.

Raging Sea
The water in the nearby Bay of Naples boiled as hot rocks and ash fell on its surface.

Hot ash stuck in people's throats. It got in their eye. In no time at all, their clothes were coated in a layer of ash. As quickly as they brushed it off, a new layer formed!

Everyone was terrified. One person shouted, "The gods are angry with us! It's the end of the world!" Another person prayed to the gods for help, wailing, "Have mercy on us!"

The ash piled up deeper and deeper. Soon it blocked the streets like snowdrifts. It filled rooms and caused roofs to cave in. The air became so thick with ash and choking fumes that it was impossible to breathe. The town was quickly disappearing under what looked like a blanket of gray snow.

About 2,000 people either chose to stay or were trapped in Pompeii. All of them died. Most of them suffocated or were crushed to death by falling buildings. But as many as 20,000 people managed to escape to the countryside.

In less than two days the town was buried under 15 to 20 feet (4.5–6 m) of ash and rocks. Heavy rain set the ash hard like cement. The town of Pompeii then lay sealed in its rocky tomb for the next 1,800 years.

Roman Gods
The Romans worshipped many gods and goddesses. Venus (above) was Pompeii's main goddess.

Volcanic Ash
The eruption of Vesuvius threw ash so high into the air that it landed as far away as Africa and Syria.

Burned Toast
Eighty-one loaves of bread, just ready to be eaten 2,000 years ago, were found in a baker's oven.

In 1860, the king of Italy ordered archaeologists to uncover Pompeii. As they dug away the layers of rock, they were amazed to find the town almost exactly as it was when the volcano erupted—a pile of coins lay on the counter of a tavern, pots and pans stood on a hearth, a bowl of eggs had been placed on a table.

They also found that the bodies of the Pompeiians had rotted away and left hollow shapes in the rock.

This dog lays curled up, still wearing his bronze collar and chain.

This cast shows a person as they were sitting when the volcano erupted.

The archaeologists poured wet plaster into the hollows to make models of the bodies, called casts. When the plaster had set hard, the archaeologists chipped away the surrounding rock and removed the casts. Many of them show people shielding their faces, clutching bags of jewels, or huddled together in terror.

The eruption of Vesuvius was a terrible event. But so many people and things were frozen in the moment of their destruction that today we have a priceless record of how the Romans lived at that time.

Mount Vesuvius is still an active volcano. It has erupted 40 times since 79 CE—in 1631, 18,000 people died—and most recently in 1944. Who knows when it will decide to wake up again?

Pompeii Today
Today, it is possible to walk along the streets of ancient Pompeii.

Scary Reminder
This picture of a skull is from a house in Pompeii. It was meant to remind people that they should enjoy life while they could.

Lisbon
This is Lisbon today. In 1755, 275,000 people lived in the city. It was the center of Portugal's empire, which stretched to South America.

Galleons
These huge ships brought precious cargoes such as gold, silver, silk, and spices from all over the empire.

LISBON'S GREAT QUAKE
Portugal, Southern Europe, 1755

All was peaceful in Lisbon, the capital city of Portugal. Mighty ships called galleons were moored in Lisbon's harbor, their cargoes safely delivered. The streets were nearly empty. Most people were in church for the festival of All Saints Day, when worshippers remember loved ones who have died.

In the royal chapel, King José and his family bowed their heads in prayer. Candles burned steadily on the altar, and the smell of incense filled the air.

Suddenly, there was a menacing rumble. Then another, lasting two full minutes, shook the city. It was the unmistakable shuddering of an earthquake! Church spires swayed like corn in a breeze. Inside the churches, bells clanged and chandeliers swung crazily.

Buildings tottered and then crashed to the ground, crushing the people inside.

A third tremor threw clouds of dust into the air, adding to the chaos and confusion. As the royal chapel began to crumble, the king and his family rushed outside. Hordes of people were running to the harbor to escape the falling buildings. But even there, they were soon to discover, they would not be safe.

King José I
José was king of Portugal between 1750 and 1777.

Destruction
Buildings that survived the quake were then gutted by flames.

Giant Waves
The giant waves that struck Lisbon's harbor were 50 feet (15 m) high.

When the crowds reached the harbor, they watched in horror as shock waves from the earthquake pulled the sea back for half a mile (1 km). Then the sea reared up and returned in three giant waves that smashed ships onto the shore and swept away the onlookers.

Flames raced through the city as upturned candles set fire to wooden beams from collapsed buildings. Soon the city was a raging inferno. Lisbon was almost completely destroyed.

King José and his family escaped unharmed. But 60,000 people died and only 3,000 of the city's 20,000 houses were left standing.

Priests warned that an angry God had caused the earthquake. But scientists suggested—for the first time in history—that earthquakes were the result of natural movements under the earth.

Deadly Quake
The tremors were so strong that water levels in lakes rose 1,000 miles (1,609 km) away in Scotland.

Farmers
Farmers work on the land, growing crops and herding animals.

Yellow River
The river snakes through northern China to the Yellow Sea. Its name comes from the color of the clay it carries.

RIVER OF SORROW
Northern China, 1887

Life was tough for the Chinese farmers who lived beside the mighty Yellow River. No matter how hard they worked each day in the fields below the river, they barely produced enough food to feed their families.

September 1887 saw a month of almost continuous rain. The river had begun to rise and people feared that it would burst its banks.

Over the centuries, the Yellow River had flooded the flatlands of China's Great Plain more than 1,500 times. The river had claimed so many lives and caused such tremendous suffering that it was known as "China's Sorrow."

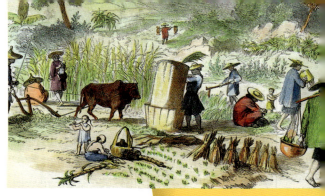

Despite the threat of flooding, no one thought to leave. It was their home, and their families had lived there for hundreds of years. And it was harvest time—they would starve if they did not bring in their crops soon.

The rain continued to fall, and the river rose higher and higher. In some places it was already 15 feet (5 m) above the surrounding flatlands. While some farmers gathered the harvest, others set to work building embankments alongside the river. These embankments, called dykes, were their only hope of holding back the water.

But it was no use. At a sharp bend near the city of Zhengzhou, the river finally swelled over its banks. It tore a gap half a mile (1 km) long in the dykes, pouring a torrent of water onto the Great Plain.

Harvest Crops
The farmers grew wheat, corn, rice, sweet potatoes, and a type of grass called sorghum.

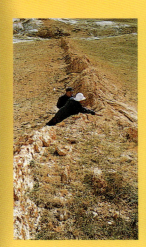

Flood Defense
For 2,500 years the Chinese have built dykes and dug channels to take the floodwater away.

Rafts
Straw and wicker rafts were similar to those used on the Yellow River today.

Disease
Drinking water that was contaminated by the flood led to disease.

Constant Threat
The river has flooded often since 1887.

The flood swept away the farmers in the fields, but their cries were unheard above the noise of the rushing water. As the torrent reached the villages beyond the river, people climbed onto their roofs for safety. Some braved the flood in boats or rafts, rescuing people or throwing food to those marooned by the raging water.

The flood covered 11 cities and 1,500 villages, and killed 900,000 people. Thousands more died of disease and starvation. It took 18 months to fix the dykes and bring the river back under control.

Today, the flood defenses along the Yellow River are much improved. Dynamite has been used to alter the river's course to avoid dangerous bends, and huge, powerful dams have been built. But the river will never be completely tamed. "China's Sorrow" will still be a force of nature.

Mount Pelée
This mountain was named after Pele, the Hawaiian goddess of volcanoes. A minor eruption 50 years before had covered the mountain with gray ash.

PELÉE AWAKES
Martinique, Caribbean, 1902

It was nearly 8:00 a.m., and the port of St. Pierre on the Caribbean island of Martinique was bustling. Sugar, rum, and bananas were being loaded onto ships, while French tourists strolled along the elegant streets. Local people toiled in the heat of the orchards and plantations.

Yet people were leaving town. Some were waiting for boats to take them off the island. Others were leaving by road. They were nervous because the usually quiet Pelée was belching smoke and ashes.

At night, red-hot cinders from Mount Pelée lit up the sky.

Governor
Louis Mouttet, the island's governor, stayed in the town to reassure people that St. Pierre was safe.

An official report had said there was no danger. But this did not stop the fear that gripped the town, and Governor Mouttet sent guards to keep more people from leaving.

Leon, the local shoemaker, watched the people leaving. He had lived here all his life and knew there was no cause for alarm.

In his jail cell, Auguste Ciparis wasn't concerned either. Locked away, without even a window, he knew nothing of events in the town.

Prisoner
Auguste Ciparis had been found guilty of murder and sentenced to death.

Stopped Watch
This watch melted to a stop at 8:15 a.m.

Bloodthirsty
The harbor at St. Pierre filled with hungry sharks attracted by the dead bodies floating in the water.

Suddenly Mount Pelée exploded with a sound like a thousand cannons firing. A glowing cloud of white-hot steam, dust, and gas rolled down the mountain— heading straight for St. Pierre!

The suffocating air killed most people instantly. Some tried to escape, but they were overtaken by the rapidly moving cloud.

The shoemaker staggered into his house, clutching his chest. His lungs were racked with pain, and his skin was burning. He threw himself onto his bed, expecting to die. All around him things began to melt in the heat.

The streets ran with burning rum from flattened warehouses. Ships in the harbor capsized and sank as the fiery blast swept over them. In a matter of seconds, St. Pierre was reduced to a flaming ruin.

Glass bottle

Melting
Temperatures reached 1800°F (1000°C), melting objects like the bottle above.

Amazingly, Leon survived. But rescuers found no one else alive. Then, after four days, a faint cry was heard. Digging hard, they found Ciparis buried in the rubble of the prison. The thick walls of his cell had saved his life! He was later pardoned and granted his freedom.

The eruption of Pelée was the 20th century's worst volcanic disaster. Only two people survived. The rest of St. Pierre's 30,000 citizens were wiped out in a few minutes.

Iron nails

Spoon and fork

27

San Francisco
The city began as a shanty town and grew after the gold rush of the mid 1800s.

Chinatown
The largest Chinese community outside of China itself lived in Chinatown.

EARTHQUAKE!
SAN FRANCISCO, CALIFORNIA, 1906

Dawn was breaking over the city of San Francisco. Two tourists named Carl and Pedro were strolling back to their hotel after enjoying the nightlife in the city's Chinatown district.

The two friends were joking and chatting about the evening's fun. "What a night we've had!" said Pedro, laughing. Suddenly, Carl seemed to hurl himself against a wall. "Hey! Stop fooling around!" shouted Pedro. Then he, too, was thrown off-balance as the earth shook and heaved beneath his feet.

Bricks and broken glass showered down as buildings began to tilt and sway. "It's a quake, it's a quake!" cried a terrified man as he ran past.

Screams could be heard above the loud rumbling and grinding of the earthquake, as people fled their collapsing houses. Most were still dressed in their pajamas.

The tremors ended in a few minutes. Carl and Pedro looked around and saw that whole streets had been flattened by the earthquake. Even City Hall, which was supposed to be shockproof, had been shaken to pieces.

City Hall
The dome of the hall was left standing on a skeleton of girders.

Tremors
The main earth tremor lasted one minute and five seconds.

Ham and Eggs Fire
One of the worst fires was called the "Ham and Eggs Fire." It began when a woman cooked breakfast in her shattered home.

Fire Trucks
The city's 38 horse-drawn fire trucks were no match for the 52 separate fires that broke out in San Francisco.

30

Earthquakes were nothing new to the people of San Francisco. The city sits on a great crack in the Earth's surface called the San Andreas Fault. Two chunks of the Earth's crust, called plates, meet at this fault. These plates slide against each other, sometimes causing earthquakes.

Carl and Pedro returned to their hotel but found only a heap of rubble. All the other guests had been crushed to death when it collapsed.

But the danger had just begun.

Gas from broken pipes filled the air. Fires started as the flames from stoves and heaters, and sparks from severed electricity cables, ignited the gas. Soon whole streets were ablaze.

The water mains had shattered, too, so there was no water supply. Without water, the firefighters had to battle the blazes with sewage. Restaurant owners broke open bottles of wine to dampen the flames.

Firefighters blew up entire streets with dynamite, trying to create fire breaks—gaps between buildings to stop the flames from spreading. But the fires raged on.

Fire Breaks
Most efforts to stop the fires by blowing up buildings simply created more fires.

The fires destroyed more buildings than the earthquake did.

Looters
Thieves searched the rubble for valuables. Some looters were shot on sight by police.

Finally the fires died out. Five hundred people had been killed, and 200,000 people were left homeless. They slept on the streets or in Golden Gate Park, building shelters from whatever they could find. Some women gave birth to their babies on the grass in the park!

People searched the rubble for their belongings.

Rebuilding began immediately. Within four years, there was barely a trace of the quake's destruction.

Earthquakes still rock the city—a 1994 quake killed 61 people. But buildings are now constructed to withstand the tremors, and firefighting techniques have improved. San Francisco no longer has to be rebuilt after each earthquake.

Makeshift Stoves
People prepared their meals on temporary stoves until the electricity was restored.

Camps
Thousands of people lived in tents for up to three years after the earthquake.

Forecasting
In the 1930s, forecasters used changes in air pressure to predict hurricanes. Today they use pictures of cloud patterns taken by satellites.

Wind Speed
The hurricane traveled at 60 miles per hour (96 kph), but wind speeds inside it reached 180 miles per hour (290 kph).

Storm-Free
Long Island had not had a hurricane for 100 years.

LONG ISLAND EXPRESS
NORTHEASTERN U.S., 1938

"Forecasters from the U.S. Weather Bureau are warning that a hurricane is heading toward Florida," said the report on the radio in Janice Kelly's Long Island home.

Janice heard the report, but her mind was on other things. Long Island, on the northeast coast of the U.S., was a long way from Florida. She was thinking about the rats that were scuttling around in her basement. Janice hated rats! She could not relax until her husband got rid of them.

Down in Florida, people started boarding up their houses. Hurricanes were a common occurrence. But as they worked, the hurricane changed direction. At first it seemed to be heading out to sea, where it would cause no harm. Then it turned north.

Gathering pace, it raced toward Long Island and the New England states like an express train. When it struck, it took everyone by surprise, toppling skyscrapers and demolishing homes as if they had been crushed by a giant steamroller.

Flying Houses
In Madison, Connecticut, one house was lifted up and blown half a mile (one km), and yet not a single window was broken!

People fled from falling buildings, dodging the flying bricks.

Windy City
The force of the hurricane winds in New York was so strong that it caused the Empire State Building (above) to sway.

The first place hit was Long Island. Families were relaxing on the beach, enjoying their picnics and watching their children build sandcastles. Out at sea, the wind was whipping up huge waves. People who lived along the shore invited their friends to come and look at the big breakers.

Suddenly a wall of water 40 feet (12 m) high rose up just off shore and crashed onto the beach, sweeping everyone away.

The sea surged inland, flooding towns along the coast. People were tossed about in the floodwaters. Some were rescued by those in higher buildings, who let down bedsheets and hauled them to safety.

Hurricane winds blasted across seven states, derailing trains and splitting roads. Floodwaters set off car horns. Their blaring was added to the screams of the raging winds.

Toppled Train
This train was surrounded by seawater and began to sink. Luckily, all the passengers escaped.

Flood Damage
This road split into two when floodwater loosened soil underneath.

Wave Power
In some places, the force of the waves changed the shape of the coastline permanently.

Destruction
The winds and the tidal wave they produced destroyed more than 57,000 houses. About 275 million trees were felled.

Janice Kelly and her husband clambered onto the roof of their house to escape the rising water. They were not the only ones to seek refuge on the roof. Three rats and a snake had beaten them to it! Janice shuddered. She hated rats! But the raging storm terrified her more.

Then, with a loud ripping sound, the wind tore the roof off the house! It swirled away across the bay, with the couple still clinging on. They closed their eyes, expecting to die. Suddenly they jolted to a halt. They had come to rest on a golf course.

The Kellys looked across the bay to where their house once stood. Houses were flattened, cars were upturned and half-buried in mud, and nearly every tree had been uprooted. The roof had been a miraculous life raft for the Kellys and their animal passengers.

The hurricane devastated thousands of lives. Sixty thousand people were left homeless. The final death toll stood at more than 600. The "Long Island Express," as it was named, cut a path 325 miles (523 km) long before it finally blew itself out.

Paint Stripper
The force of the wind scratched the paint off cars and stripped painted houses down to the bare wood.

Sea Salt
Wind carried sea salt 120 miles (193 km) inland where it turned windows white.

Andes
This mountain range stretches along the entire Pacific coast of South America.

Peru's People
Many Peruvians are descendants of the ancient Inca people.

The Highest
The Andes range is slowly rising due to movements inside Earth. It may one day be the highest mountain range in the world.

AVALANCHE
Peru, South America, 1970

It was the end of May, and a group of friends from Japan were on a climbing vacation in Yungay. The town was a small but flourishing tourist resort that sat at the foot of towering Mount Huascaran in the Andes mountains of Peru. The locals, like most of soccer-mad Peru, were in the grip of World Cup fever. They had high hopes for the Peruvian team.

Each day the friends set off early to watch the sun rise over the Andes. At night, they sat under the 100-foot (30-m)-tall palm trees in the town square and watched people coming and going.

One afternoon, while the friends were out climbing, a tremendous earthquake split apart the ocean bed just off the Peruvian coast. Earth tremors rippled right across mainland Peru.

It struck 23 minutes into the first World Cup game. Most of the locals were at home, following the match.

High up on Mount Huascaran, the climbers paused to enjoy the scenery. As they looked down at the quiet town, a low rumbling began. It seemed to grow louder and louder.

Then the mountainside far beneath them started to move. As they watched in horror, a huge mass of ice and rock cascaded down the face of the mountain. It was heading right toward the town!

Speed
An avalanche can move three times faster than highway traffic.

Boulders the size of houses hurtled down the mountain, part of a deadly wall of ice, mud, and rock. As the climbers watched, the wall hit the town and buried it.

The climbers hurried down to look for survivors, but Yungay had been wiped away. All that remained visible were the tops of four of the palm trees in the town square. The only survivors were a few people who had taken refuge in a hilltop cemetery at the edge of town.

Yungay was just one of many towns and villages devastated by the earthquake. The whole world was shocked by the scale of the disaster.

A short time later, Peru won its World Cup match against Bulgaria. The success helped lift the people's spirits as they began the long task of rebuilding their shattered lives.

Rescue
It was three days before the mud was hard enough for rescuers to get to Yungay.

This statue of Jesus in the cemetery was the only thing not destroyed by the avalanche.

43

Bush
The bush is uncultivated land covered with scrub and trees.

Eucalyptus
These trees burn quickly because they have oily leaves.

WILDFIRE
Australia, 2019-2020

Wildfires are not unusual during Australia's summers. The country's hot and dry climate creates conditions that can ignite a spark and quickly send flames across the landscape. Many plants, such as the widespread eucalyptus trees, even depend on wildfires to help spread their seeds.

But 2019 brought devastating wildfires. It had been the hottest and driest year on record. Months of scorching heat and extreme drought had left the country dry as a bone.

In September, wildfires began in the southeastern part of the country. Out in the bush, dry vegetation began to smolder and then catch fire after lightning struck. Fanned by the wind, small fires grew rapidly. Trees began bursting into flames. Firefighters and groups of volunteers struggled to control the raging fire.

The fires were concentrated along the southeastern coast in New South Wales, but hit all across Australia.

By March 2020, when heavy rains helped bring the fires to an end, the smoke and flames had killed more than 445 people and burned an estimated 98.3 million acres (39 million hectares). An estimated three billion animals died or were displaced.

Changing Color
Smoke and ash from the fires caused New Zealand's snowcapped mountains and glaciers to turn brown.

Helpful Dogs
Service dogs helped find koalas and other wildlife whose forest homes had burned down.

GLOSSARY

Archaeologist
An expert who digs up ancient remains and tries to work out what happened in the past

Avalanche
A huge fall of rock, ice, and snow from the side of a mountain

Bush
An open, uncultivated area of grasses, shrubs, and trees

Crust
The Earth's outer layer, made up of huge slabs of rock that rest on a bed of liquid rock

Drought
A long period with very little rain or no rain at all

Dyke
A wall built alongside a river or canal to hold back floodwater

Earthquake
A shaking of the ground caused by movement of the segments that make up the topmost layer of the Earth

Eruption
The explosion of a volcano, which may throw out lava, steam, ash, dust, suffocating fumes, and hot gas

Forecaster
A scientist who studies the weather and predicts how it will change

Hurricane
A terrible storm with a swirling mass of powerful winds at its center

Lava
Red-hot liquid rock from inside the Earth that bursts onto the surface

Monsoon
The rainy season in tropical regions

Natural disaster
A destructive event caused by the forces of nature

Plain
A large expanse of level land in the open country

Plates
Segments of the Earth's crust. These large slabs of rock cover the Earth's surface like a giant jigsaw puzzle.

Skyscraper
A tall building consisting of many stories, usually built of concrete and steel

Tremor
A trembling of the ground. Earthquakes are usually made up of a number of powerful tremors, coming one after the other.

Volcano
A mountain with a central crater through which hot gases, ash, and molten rock sometimes burst out

INDEX

Andes mountains 40–43

ash
  New Zealand 45
  Pompeii 10–13

Australia 7, 44–45

avalanches
  Peru 6, 40–43
  speed of 41

bush 7, 44

bushfires 7, 44–45

camps, temporary 33

casts, plaster 14, 15

China's Sorrow 20, 22

Ciparis, Auguste 25, 27

dykes 21

earthquakes
  Lisbon 6, 16–19
  Peruvian coast 40–41, 43
  San Francisco 6, 28–33

Empire State Building, New York 35

eucalyptus trees 44

farmers, Chinese 20, 21, 22

fire breaks 31

firefighters
  Australia 44
  San Francisco 30–31

fires
  Australia 44–45
  Lisbon 6, 18
  San Francisco 30–31

floods
  Long Island 37
  Yellow River 7, 20–23

forecasters 34

galleons 16

gods and goddesses 12, 13, 19, 24

Great Plain, China 20, 21

Huascaran, Mount, Peru 40–43

hurricanes
  Long Island 6, 34–39
  winds 7, 34, 35, 37, 38, 39

José I, King of Portugal 16, 17, 19

Kelly, Janice 34, 38–39

lava flow 7

Leon the shoemaker 25, 26, 27

Lisbon, Portugal 6, 16–19

Long Island, New York 6, 34–39

looters 32

Madison, Connecticut 35

Martinique, Caribbean 6, 24–27

Mount Huascaran, Peru 40–43

Mount Pelée, Martinique 6, 24–27

Mount St. Helens, Washington State 10

Mount Vesuvius, Italy 7, 8–15

Mouttet, Governor 25

Pele (goddess) 24

Pelée, Mount, Martinique 6, 24–27

plates, of the Earth 30

Pliny 11

Pompeii, Italy 7, 8–15
  amphitheater 9
  bodies 14–15
  gladiators 9

St. Helens, Mount, Washington State 10

St. Pierre, Martinique 6, 24–27

San Andreas Fault 30

San Francisco, California
  Chinatown 28
  City Hall 29
  earthquake 6, 28–33
  Golden Gate Park 32
  Ham and Eggs Fire 30

sea salt 39

service dogs 45

tremors 16, 17, 19, 28–30, 40

Venus (goddess) 13

volcanoes
  Mount Pelée 6, 24–27
  Mount Vesuvius 7, 8–15

waves, giant 18, 37

wildfires 44-45

winds, hurricane 7, 34, 35, 37, 38, 39

World Cup 40, 41, 43

Yellow River, China 7, 20–23

Yungay, Peru 6, 40–43

47

QUIZ

Answer the questions to see what you have learned. Check your answers in the key below.

1. Where is Mount Vesuvius?
2. True or False: The earthquake in Lisbon, Portugal, caused giant waves to crash onto shore.
3. What did the farmers build to try and hold back the floodwaters from the Yellow River?
4. What natural disaster hit St. Pierre?
5. What is the name of the crack in Earth's surface on which the city of San Francisco sits?
6. What was the hurricane called that blew through Long Island, New York?
7. What caused the avalanche on Mount Huascaran in Peru?
8. What caused the wildfires in Australia?

1. Near Pompeii, Italy 2. True 3. Embankments, or dykes
4. Mount Pelée erupted 5. San Andreas Fault 6. Long Island Express
7. An earthquake 8. Heat and extreme drought